Eight Secrets to What Makes Great Beer

The Insider's Guide to Craft Brewing and Beer

By T.A & P.A Harris

© Copyright 2023 - All rights reserved.

The content contained within this book may not be reproduced, duplicated or transmitted without direct written permission from the author or the publisher.

Under no circumstances will any blame or legal responsibility be held against the publisher, or author, for any damages, reparation, or monetary loss due to the information contained within this book, either directly or indirectly.

Legal Notice:

This book is copyright protected. It is only for personal use. You cannot amend, distribute, sell, use, quote or paraphrase any part, or the content within this book, without the consent of the author or publisher.

Disclaimer Notice:

Please note the information contained within this document is for educational and entertainment purposes only. All effort has been executed to present accurate, up to date, reliable, complete information. No warranties of any kind are declared or implied. Readers acknowledge that the author is not engaged in the rendering of legal, financial, medical or professional advice. The content within this book has been derived from various sources. Please consult a licensed professional before attempting any techniques outlined in this book.

By reading this document, the reader agrees that under no circumstances is the author responsible for any losses, direct or indirect, that are incurred as a result of the use of the information contained within this document, including, but not limited to, errors, omissions, or inaccuracies.

Table of Contents

INTRODUCTION 1

THE NUTS AND BOLTS OF A BREWERY 5

SECRET 1: CLEANLINESS.. 11

SECRET 2: WATER 17

SECRET 3: MALT.. 23

SECRET 4: HOPS 29

SECRET 5: YEAST 41

SECRET 6: TEMPERATURE.. 49

SECRET 7: TIME.. 59

SECRET 8: RECIPE 71

CONCLUSION 81

EXAMPLE RECIPES 87

GLOSSARY OF TERMS 107

THE END 113

Introduction

Why We Wanted to Write This Book

The term passionate beer lovers or beer enthusiasts is certainly one that applies to both me and my dad. My dad really is Mr. Beer, originally an award-winning keeper of fine beer, famed by his iconic beer festivals with nearly 100 beers at the Brunswick Inn. One of the first true free houses with beers from far and wide, across the 17 hand pulls on offer every-day. Then becoming a brewer in his own right and now with more awards than you can shake a stick at. He has founded two breweries, the first bringing brewing back to his hometown by being the first modern day brewery in the city of Derby.

Me, I have of course grown up in and around beer. Working in pubs as the son of a landlord, behind the bar from the age of 14, and working my first brew day significantly before that, getting acquitted with one of the secrets of great beer, cleaning! Since then, I have travelled, always seeking the best beers wherever I go. I went on to work for several high-profile drinks companies until returning to work in and ultimately run the family business, growing our award-winning pub and brewing business. As you would expect in any small business I have been involved in all aspects and really know what it takes to deliver consistent great beer and great pubs, it's really become a passion of mine. I have lost count of the beers I have sampled over the years. Although the market and the beer in it have changed immeasurably in that time, the fundamentals that make great beer have been retained.

It was against this backdrop that I was looking for a Christmas present for my dad—a beer book I thought would be the perfect swap out for the evening paper. Only to find the beer and brewing books on the market were more like textbooks. Seriously, they actually have tables, graphs and equations; a throw-back to chemistry rather than the light-hearted, entertaining beer book I was looking for. Great for those super detail-oriented readers, written by academics focusing on the science behind brewing, but not much of an evening or poolside read! I discussed this with my dad, who went from being a landlord to an accomplished national award-winning brewer, by learning in the brewhouse, with the help of brewing consultant Chris Marchbanks, rather than in the classroom. So, we thought why don't we write a book aimed at genuine beer enthusiasts that love beer, using lessons and anecdotes from our decades of award-winning experience in a commercial brewhouse. We run hugely popular brewery tours where people just love to understand more about beer and of course chat about all things beer over a few pints—let's face it who doesn't! One guy's been on the tour five times although we suspect the generous quantities of beer might have something to do with it.

It was this we wanted to replicate but in book form.

The more we talked the more we decided we had to do it, focusing on what makes great beer, creating our very own brewery tour in a book. Perfect for those that just love beer, like us, or someone interested in those real-life commercial brewing anecdotes from my dad's decades in the brewhouse, maybe at the start of their beer or brewing journey.

So, why not grab yourself a beer and join us as we enter the world of beer, learning what we believe makes a great beer.

Cheers,

Paul & Trev

4

The Nuts and Bolts of

a Brewery

A Guide Around the Brewhouse

Before getting into the secrets of what makes great beer it's important to understand the mechanics of a commercial brewery, well at least all the hand craft breweries we have operated. So here are the 12 main stages of the brew process, with a helpful visual representation of each vessel.

Step 1: Milling Our Malt

This is quite unusual for a smaller brewery as most buy in ready milled malt. We have always freshly milled our malt. The process involves milling or gently crushing the malt so the hard shell on the malt is broken and it's ready for mashing. Essentially allowing the brew water to infuse those malt flavours into the mash water, which forms the basis of the wort and then beer. We have always milled our malt within 12 hours of a brew, this way just like freshly ground coffee beans, it ensures we get the most flavour from our malts, which include some of the most expensive the world has to offer.

Step 2: Mashing

Mashing is the process of adding the freshly milled malt to 66-degree water. For smaller scale hand-crafted breweries like ours, the mixture is literally hand turned by paddle until a thick porridge is formed. Trust me, when you're brewing a dark beer with over 12 malts, it's a real workout!

Step 3: Sparging

Once the porridge has been allowed time to rest and that lovely malt flavour infuses with the water you begin the sparging process. In effect, sprinkling 66-degree water over the top of the malt to keep it moist, although not too much—more on this later.

Step 4: Run Off

This is running off the wort prior to the fermentation process which converts those sugars into alcohol, creating beer. Wort is the name given to the malt infused water which forms the basis of the soon to be beer. Run off is transferring the wort from the Mash Tun into the copper via the underback. The Mash Tun valve is opened to fill the large stainless-steel bath (the underback). As each bath is filled this is then pumped directly into the copper. Once the coils of the copper are covered with the wort, the copper is switched on, to begin heating up the wort.

Step 5 and Step 6: The Copper and the Boil

The copper itself is simply a giant stainless-steel kettle, where the lovely ingredients are all boiled up. Initially the bittering hops are added and later the aroma hops are added. The aroma hops are added toward the end of the boil, so not to boil them all away. As the name suggests these contribute to the aroma of the beer—more on this later.

Step 7: Hop Back

This is housed in the underback, the same stainless-steel bath used to transfer the wort during run off. Initially the wort is transferred to the underback. The hop basket which is housed in the underback is filled with the recipe's chosen dry hopping hops. It is then allowed to soak, to ensure these hop flavours infuse into the wort. All the remaining wort passes through these hops, throughout the transfer process from the copper to the fermentation vessel (FV) via the paraflow, to bring down the temperature.

Step 8: Cooling the Wort

Prior to transfer to the FV, it is essential to cool the wort down to 20 degrees as the yeast will not work at higher temperatures. Cooling of the wort takes place via the paraflow or heat exchanger which is, in effect, a backwards radiator. The hot wort is passed through the system, and although not coming directly into contact with the water, the proximity of the pipework brings the temperature down to the 20 degrees required for fermentation to take place.

Step 9: Oxygenate

Oxygenating the wort is the process of adding oxygen to the wort to ensure the yeast kicks off its fermentation quickly, as yeast feeds off the sugars and oxygen.

Step 10: Fermentation

This is where the magic happens, converting those sugars to alcohol and creating beer!

Step 11: Raking Tanks

Once the beer has fermented out, it is transferred to the raking tanks, again an unusual process in smaller breweries. Many brewers will barrel directly from FV, however, raking from raking tanks really helps with beer clarity and removing unwanted yeast and sediment from the beer.

Step 12: Barrelling

Exactly what it says on the tin, filling up those barrels with delicious beer!

Secret 1:

Cleanliness

Qualify as a Cleaner Before You Qualify as a Brewer

In a brewery cleanliness is everything. I have always said you qualify as a cleaner before you qualify as a brewer. My motto used to be, "Clean and then when you think you're satisfied, clean it again just to be sure." When I started out it was really a case of scrubbing every inch of the stainless-steel until it talks to you. Physically getting into every part of the brewery that the beer comes into contact with. Climbing into the vessels; cleaning and scrubbing them until the water that comes out is crystal clear.

Today it's more a combination of old-fashioned elbow grease with the help of CIP Spray Balls, which in effect blast the vessels clean. Helping to reduce workload from the initial cleaning process, this initial clean removes the dirt and spent ingredients from the plant, until seemingly clean. In most cases it's easy to see if the vessel is clean, as the water coming out is crystal clear when rinsed down. This is then followed by sterilising chemicals. CIP Spray Balls replace much of the physical scrubbing and are then followed with chemicals to allow you to get in to those hard-to-reach nooks and crannies. Originally, I was sceptical on the chemical front, however, we have proven that it simply improves the process. We now use a combination of caustic which is run through the cleaned brewing plant after every brew. Following the full route the wort would follow on the brew day to ensure that nothing can survive in the plant. We then use peracetic acid to further sterilise items just prior to use. The beauty of peracetic acid is once dry, it simply evaporates leaving all parts of the brewery and equipment fully sterile and ready for use.

This has to apply to every area the wort or finished beer comes into contact with. You can brew the best beer in the world, following consistency in every other part of the process, however, if there are elements of the brewery that are not clean then quite simply you are wasting your time. A good example is cask cleaning. This can be a monotonous job and is often an entry level task in any commercial brewery. However, if the casks are not properly cleaned then the beer will be ruined at the last stage.

Over the years there have been many new breweries who have not taken cleanliness seriously enough. In fact, many in the industry won't purchase from a new brewery until they have been brewing consistently for 12 months, as within this timeframe it will be clear if they have the required hygiene standards. Cleanliness in a brewery can often have a cumulative impact, building over time. It can lead to unintended changes to the flavour profile of your beers, off flavours to the taste, but noticeable particularly on the nose, and creating issues in terms of beer clarity. All of which mean your beers are not consistent. This will also put off perspective landlords and drinkers, causing huge reputational damage that has killed off some breweries before they have even really started.

In essence, without cleanliness it's very difficult to have consistency. When I started out this was something some of the larger established brewers would throw at us smaller brewers. They were seemingly unimpressed with the growing number of new entrants in the market; they would argue that smaller brewers do not have consistency in their beers. Many of us early microbreweries, as we were referred to then, proved this was quite simply not the case.

To achieve this, you had to be consistent in terms of your process, accurately recording and weighing out every element of your recipe and only making any small adjustments one at a time or as needed. For example, with a new malt harvest, to ensure same taste or colour profile to your beers, you would need to tweak the grist on the advice of the maltster as each year's harvest can vary slightly.

Generally, this would mean repeating your recipe to the letter, documenting it with each brew, following the same process time and time again, brew after brew after brew. In essence you can't cut corners, and cleanliness is the same. You can be completely consistent in all other aspects but if you don't have cleanliness then those off flavours and clarity issues will destroy your beer, removing any consistency. Which in many ways is what those larger brewers were getting at, as they just didn't believe beer would be brewed with the same professionalism and diligence they apply. They just didn't believe it could be achieved at our scale— something I'm proud to have helped prove wasn't the case.

I have always said brewing and beer has an incredible way of getting under the skin. The passion for beer must be there. That's what gets you out of bed at silly o'clock in the morning and knowing it's a beer day still gives me the same kick it did all those years ago. However, I truly believe that to be a great brewer and brew great beer you must get a kick out of scrubbing and cleaning vessels, just as much as you do by creating an amazing beer. I have taught many people to brew over the years and I have always had the same enthusiasm for cleanliness as the more seemingly glamorous parts of brewing. So, I'd jump in and show them, influencing them to pick up those great habits. Unfortunately, the knees won't allow me to do that anymore.

I have often been asked if I have ever had to throw a beer away. I can honestly say that no I have never had to, even in all the years of brewing, across the thousands and thousands of brews. I think that is as much down to a consistent approach to brewing and cleanliness as anything else. However, I have made one mistake when brewing our best-selling beer Business as Usual, a 4.4% amber beer. Back in the early days I fermented the beer out at 5% rather than the intended 4.4%. So Old Accidental was born, which later became Old Intentional. Ultimately creating an award-winning beer. I later changed the name but not the recipe, as at that point a few years down the line, having been brewing for so many years, I should have known what I was doing. So, we made a positive out of it. Like anything in brewing and life you will of course make mistakes, but it's about owning it and making a positive from the situation. In terms of brewing, it's the process that protects you. With consistency the mistakes will be few and far between. When it comes to brewing great beer, I can't emphasise enough just how important consistent cleanliness is. You have to be a cleaner; you have to be a really good cleaner, then you'll make a good brewer, which is essential if you are to brew a great beer!

16

Secret 2:

Water

It Takes 7–8 Pints of Water to Produce Just One Pint of Beer

The single largest ingredient in every beer you produce, or drink is always the water, accounting for an amazing 95% of it. So, it is not surprising that it has a huge impact on the finished beer, much more than many realise. There are many high-profile examples in the industry. It's also not just the water in the beer that's needed to produce beer but due to the rigorous cleaning process, cooling, and many more tasks it actually takes seven to eight pints of water to create just one pint of beer!

What's in Your Water

The starting point for great beer therefore has to be the water. It is important to test the water prior to brewing, as it varies so much in terms of mineral make up across the country. We have always used Murphy & Son, our local brew chemist to regularly test the water. Their focus is on the mineral content and the suitability of the water for brewing, in order to form a solid base that is suitable for brewing. Once determined they would then produce an addition called DWB (blend of minerals to make the water optimal for brewing), which is added to the mash water just prior to the mash in, when the milled malt is added to the water. What's missing in most cases is calcium to create the optimal water for brewing. The water in Burton on Trent has calcium naturally (it isn't added), hence it being the historic home of brewing as their water content is considered the perfect base for brewing beer; so much so that this process is in fact called Burtonizing your water.

Most brewers simply use the tap water in their location to brew with, so the water authority would be relied upon to ensure the water is safe to use. There are however a few brewers around the country that instead use well water if they are fortunate to have a well on their land. Just as I did at the Brunswick Inn, where when building a traditional tower style brewery, we discovered a well, right in line with the boundary wall, leading to the wall becoming curved to wrap around the well with the addition of a spiral staircase. Again, we used Murphy & Son but this time they had to test the water for cleanliness as well as suitability for brewing. They were happy with the water, and we brewed with that well water for many years, of course regularly testing the water. It was only when major works took place locally, to build a fly over to a new business park, that the well water was disturbed, and we had to switch to tap water. I was paranoid that this would change the beer, but there was no change to the beer. I should have realised as the make-up of the water was almost identical, but I guess I had become influenced by the romanticism of using well water. It just shows water is determined by its location above all else.

Location, Location, Location

In addition to the calcium content of water, the water in many areas is particularly distinctive, hence the beers from these locations are easily recognisable in terms of flavour profiles. Cornwall or Scotland are good examples of this, an indication of just how much impact water has on the finished beer.

It is also why beer just doesn't travel well when breweries are bought out by larger competitors, and they decide to move the location of where the beer is brewed. Seemingly following the recipe to the letter but with one huge difference, they can't change the water. One such example was when W&D, or Bankies as they used to be known, purchased Marston's. They had a huge beer factory, as we would call it, with capacity in Wolverhampton and wanted to move production there, as it would be more cost effective. At the time I sold large amounts of Pedigree Marston's best-selling beer in the Brunswick Inn, the brew pub I ran. I put the beer up on stillage, as usual, and of course tasted the beer prior to putting it on the bar. It never made it that far. It was a nice pint, but it was not Pedigree. I even blind tasted with several regular pedigree drinkers just to be sure. I gave them each a sample of the beer and said, "What do you think?" They all agreed it was a nice pint. I said, "What would you say if I told you it was pedigree?" They simply said, "If you think that's pedigree you must have been drinking!" I called the brewery, and a representative came out. He tested the beer and poured every barrel down the drain—it was over 1,000 pints! When I asked him why it wasn't being used, as it's still a nice beer, he simply said, "My instructions were to dump it and say nothing." After this I went from a regular order of over 1,000 pints to no longer ordering any. Around two months later I received a phone call from Paul Bailey, the Head Brewer of Marston's and a friend of mine. He said, "Trev, what's this I hear? You don't have Pedigree on the bar?" My response, more to the point: "Do you have any Pedigree at your end?" The phone went quiet. He said, "Give me two weeks and I'll send you two 18-gallon casks, complementary." We sampled the beer, and it was like it always was—Pedigree was back, clearly brewed back in Burton.

Of course, in terms of Pedigree it's not simply the water that changed by moving the brewing to Wolverhampton. The brewing process uses the old Burton Union System, a wood barrel fermentation system. Following the takeover and the roll out of the beer across their much larger pub estate the Marston's brewery in Burton could not produce enough beer from the old plant. So, they mixed a smaller percentage from the Burton plant into the beer which was produced on scale in Wolverhampton. All of this would of course affect the taste of the beer, as I experienced all those years ago. It has recently been announced that the old Burton Union system will be closed. A famous old process which adds a unique dimension to Pedigree and coined the term made in wood. So, in Pedigree's case it was not just the water. The union system enabled all the yeast to be reused for future brews, with the addition of the flavours picked up from the wood. Like the oak ageing process in whiskey production. So, this change will of course further change Pedigree forever. In reality this process was started all those years ago, when over 1,000 pints went down the drain at the Brunswick and the mixing of the Wolverhampton brewed beer with that produced at the Burton. As the Marston's marketing used to say, without the wood there is no pedigree, sadly this has come to pass in more ways than one.

Another more standard example of the impact of moving beer production and therefore the water you brew with was the once lovely brewery, Jennings. Originally based in the beautiful Lake District, again purchased by W&D or the newly rebranded Marston's. In a sadly familiar story, Jennings's beers are also now produced in the same beer factory in Wolverhampton. In fact, the old historic brewery has now been sold off, so unfortunately the name is the same but nothing else.

Sadly, this seems to be happening by the day now as the brewing industry continues to unwind from the impact of Covid and continued challenges. In fact, as I write this it has been announced that Breal group, owners of Back Sheep, having recently 'saved' Brew by Numbers and Brick Brewery will close their London breweries and move brewing to the consolidated Black Sheep brewery in Yorkshire. Sadly, the end of these excellent London brands. Leading inevitably to fundamental changes to the beers, as they are moved geographically to yet another beer factory for production.

This just shows the dangers of harmonisation of the beer market and the huge impact water has on the finished product. It demonstrates the importance when you are setting up a brewery of getting this right. If you are to create a great beer, you must take time to truly understand the make-up of the water in your region. It is essential you use a good brew chemist like Murphy & Son to assess your single biggest ingredient and point you in the right direction, to ensure your water is the foundation you need. If you do this then you can produce wonderful beers anywhere, without doubt. So, it's not a stumbling block but simply something that has to be part of your preparation for brewing and, of course, it needs to be part of your regular checks. Moving a beer on the other hand isn't quite so simple.

Secret 3:

Malt

The Foundation and Body of Any Great Beer

For me, without a doubt, malt forms the foundation and body of any great beer. Hops are always seen as the fashionable ingredient that drinkers and the industry are always talking about and putting on a pedestal. Now many hops are sought out by drinkers and used to sell beers. After all, we have all heard of Citra and the other high-profile hops. However, without getting your combination of your grist of malts right, your beer will be lacking, and no combination of hops can pull you through.

It is very clear for me that in order to brew a great beer you can't compromise on your malt if you want to have a beer with body and balance—more on this in the recipe section. In addition to giving your beer its body, malt will also dictate the colour of your beer. It's important to understand the variety of malt available to a brewer and ultimately what a maltster does and why they are so important in the process of making great beer.

The Maltsters Role

My advice to anyone setting up a brewery would be to find a great maltster and put your faith in them. Maltsters produce malts for the industry and its essential to have a good one; they are experts in their field and will even come out to set up your mill to ensure you are really getting the most from their malt.

The maltster role is initially to germinate the barley, soaking it with water to allow a short germination process. Once the maltster is satisfied with this initial phase of the process the malt is dried in controlled conditions. It is this process that creates the fermentable sugars, which are ultimately converted into alcohol. With the base malt then roasted to higher temperatures to darken the malt and add toasted flavours or roasted flavours of toffee, biscuit and even cocoa or coffee flavours. This roasting process leads to the variety of flavours and colours available to a brewer, but you have to be wary in terms of balance, as some malts will dominate the beer if too higher percentage is used. In effect, the longer the malts are roasted the deeper the flavour and colour of the malt.

If your maltster happens to be a traditional floor maltings then you will be head and shoulders above the rest from the start. This is the traditional way of malting barley. The barley is spread across a heated floor and turned by hand using what can only be described as a plough tool. It adds extra cost but it's without doubt the best malt you can buy. Only a few traditional floor maltings remain in the UK, Germany and Czech

Republic, unsurprising given the brewing heritage of these countries and value placed on the quality of malt by their brewers.

The Malts in a Brewer's Armoury

Without a doubt the finest malt in the world, with a price tag to match, is Maris Otter. It has won more awards than any other malt for a reason. I believe that you can't compromise on your malt; I can always taste a beer that's not made using Maris Otter malt. This is why 95% of the beers I brew all contain Maris Otter, plus we freshly mill our malt to ensure we get the most flavour possible—more on this later.

Malt can go from very pale straw colour, which would produce a lager colour beer, using lager malts or low colour Maris Otter for example, as you may find in a Pilsner. The next along the spectrum would be your pale of golden ales which would be predominantly Maris Otter, adding more body but only slightly deeper in colour.

Then the amber style beers, such our own Business as Usual, would use more of the crystal type 200 malts to add body and the deeper colour resulting in the more toffee like flavours, a middle ground if you like.

You would then be moving into brown ale territory as you include your type 400 crystal malts and chocolate malts, with that extra coffee and caramel flavour. When it comes to crystal malt the higher number simply means the barley has been roasted for longer and, as such, is deeper in colour and flavour. I find these brown ales and ruby beers really satisfying to brew, especially that feeling of putting your nose over the Mash Tun on a cold winter's day. They produce beers that are like a warm hug next to the fire—that maltiness, as I like to call it.

Finally, you move into your chocolate malts, deep brown and black in colour used in Porters and Stouts. It's the duration of heat that determines where the malt is found on the colour spectrum.

I have always used Maris Otter as the base of my beers to ensure body across all beer styles. There is more licence to add crystal type 200 and 400 as you come down the colour spectrum, moving into your amber beers and beyond. As you progress deeper in colour the world is your oyster when you get down to the porters and stouts.

I have always believed that a great dark beer should be packed full of flavour and body, so we use over 12 malts in ours. We have all had the disappointment of drinking a dark beer when it's thin and lacks body. A great beer can never lack body to that extent but it will be especially noticeable in a dark beer. I have always believed that malt is not just the basis of the colour of your beer but the foundation and base of your recipe; it must be solid before adding anything else.

One of the most common mistakes when it comes to the dark beer market is roast barley which has genuinely created more problems in the dark beer market than anything else. When it comes to a dark beer people see chocolate, black and roast barley and see them as similar. After all roasted barley is the exact colour, you are looking for in the dark beer. The issue is used to excess, and it completely dominates the beer creating a claw-like aftertaste, overpowering your beer. It must be used sparingly; you must get the percentage right.

Maximising Your Malt Flavour

Malt is always one of the most expensive ingredients in your recipe and there's only one way to get the most out of it, by milling your malt fresh prior to brewing. I have always milled mine fresh, no more than 12 hours before a brew. Malt is just like a coffee bean, the sooner you brew with it freshly milled, the more flavour you get into your beer. This is unusual for a brewery of our size, as many buy pre-milled malt, so it's not uncommon to be brewing with malt that is often three weeks old. The milling process is simply lightly crushing the malt case to allow the water to infuse during the mash and the flavour of the malt to be extracted. It also means that it's, in effect, been opened so it's losing its flavour as time passes.

So, the only way to ensure the maximum flavour from your malt is to brew with freshly milled malt.

The Beer Always Reflects What's Gone Into It

So, taking all of that into account, I don't believe that you can make a great beer without using quality malts. For me, in most cases, that means the finest malt, Maris Otter, and if you can use this malt freshly milled then you will simply get the most from it. Beer is not unlike cooking, you really do get out of it what you put in, or in malt's case, what you pay for. Cheaper malt will simply mean your beer will lack body. This is a major issue if you are producing a malty style beer, as this is the design, but also in hop forward beers as there is nothing to balance those exciting hop flavours against.

Secret 4:

Hops

The Glamour Ingredient

The section many of you will have been waiting for and without doubt the most talked about and glamourous ingredient that goes into beer—hops. It is probably because there are just so many great varieties of hops, which are so distinctive, that people develop a real love of beers which showcase their favourite hops. Combined with beers being marketed as containing certain hops in much the same way 'New World Wines' are sold by grape varietal, such as Sauvignon Blanc. However, before we get into hops and their combinations, it is important to understand how hops are used and at what stages in the brewing process.

Bittering

Hops are added at three stages in any brew. The first stage is the bittering hop. These, as the name suggests, are for bittering and are added in the early stages of the boil. As these hops are boiled for the longest period, they would not be your well-known fruity hops as the fruity flavour profiles would be all be lost in the boil. In some ways they are the essential cog in any great beer.

To give it a football analogy they are the Claude Makelele or Declan Rice of any team. They form the basis of the beer, the core, but don't get put on the pedestal that the fruity hops do, or the Lionel Messi to continue the football analogy. So, to use these hops as a bittering hop would be a waste of a beautiful hop and hence the reason you don't see Messi playing at right back.

Aroma

The second stage is the aroma hops. These are added at the very end of the boil. These are for the aroma of the beer, so more fruity varieties can be used. Due to the late stage of the boil more of the characteristics of these hops are retained in the aroma of the beer.

Dry Hop

Finally, the dry hop. This can be applied at three different times; during the collection process via the hop back in what I like to call a consistent dry hop; once fermentation is well underway in the fermentation vessel (FV) itself; or directly into the cask. Particularly in hop forward beers it can be a combination of these techniques. The dry hop in FV or in the cask are the most powerful ways of passing the hop flavours into the beer and introducing the citrussy, fruity flavours that have made hops so revered.

As an example of this, I have used Citra as a single aroma hop, combined with Fuggles and Goldings as bittering hops. The two bittering hops work brilliantly together and are perfectly suited for this, and Citra adds a fantastic aroma. On the other hand, if you were to use Citra as your bittering hop you nullify or lose most of its best characteristics, which would be literally boiled out. Losing those flavours and hop oils just isn't the ideal for a wonderful hop like Citra. Citra is of course meant to be used as an Aroma hop and comes into its own when dry hopped.

Dry hopping is a powerful way to add those flavours into your beer. Traditionally the hops were added into the cask. Which is where the term dry hopping comes from. There's a reason for this. Simply, it works. It really works, but the challenge is to make sure you are putting the same quantity of hops into each cask. To get consistency, which as we now know is crucial to brewing great beer. This can be time consuming and challenging. I have found that by adding the hops into the hop basket, which is housed in the underback, this allows you to pass all the wort through those hops. Meaning that every pint is consistently dry hopped.

The reason is that if you dry hop in cask, both the quantity of hops used and the time the beer is in cask can really start to alter the flavour of the beer. So, if you have a landlord that prefers to age his beer in his cellar, for say 6 weeks, that will make a huge difference to the beer compared to a pub that sells the beer straight from delivery.

Again, if you dry hop in a fermentation vessel for a set time period, you remain in control of the finished beer, as every pint is then exactly the same, leading to consistency. Typically, you would dry hop in FV after three or four days of the fermentation process. Both dry hopping in FV or cask would be used in addition to the consistent dry hop, as I call it, to really develop the hop flavours for a hop forward beer.

The Crystal Ball

What many people don't know when it comes to hops is that it feels like you need a crystal ball. At times as you must preorder your hops, and in some cases, this is several years in advance. It is standard to preorder your hops on a three-year hop agreement with your hop merchant, all in advance. Which is challenging in several ways, as in effect, you are predicting the style of beers that will be popular and the quantity of beer you will be brewing. No mean feat in the fast-changing beer market. You must be sensible as you are committing to the purchase of these hops financially. One of the most expensive ingredients in any beer.

There is some flexibility but less so when it comes to getting hold of very popular hops or if there has been a poor harvest. Harvests can be affected by some of the recent freak weather conditions and political upheaval we have seen across the world. In some cases, it is possible to substitute very similar hops with the same profile or alpha content.

Hops are all rated on their percentage alpha rating, for example, low alpha 2.5%–6%, dual purpose varieties 6–10%, high alpha bittering hops 10–15% and super alpha bittering 14–18%. Although there are some varieties even higher than this. As such the alpha is effectively the strength of flavour/bittering of the hop. It is also important to consider the cohumulone level of the hop, as this is an indication of the harshness of the bitterness.

Your hop merchant will provide all of the hop analysis you need and, of course, offer advice when developing recipes or substituting any unavailable hops. It is important to take this analysis and their advice into account, as this could significantly change your beer's profile. When it comes to the art of the hop order, you should keep up with emerging hops and work with your hop merchant but, in many cases, you have to just follow your gut instinct and go for it.

This was exactly the case with the emergence of perhaps the most iconic hop in recent years. Citra burst onto the beer scene and a certain UK brewery got there before anyone else. Oakham really did a great job on Oakham Citra. So much so, that most likely after tasting the finished beer, they preordered almost all of the UK supply. At that time, they really did have Citra on lock down. In fact, it took me nearly four years to finally get hold of some Citra hops! When the phone call finally came that we could have some Citra that's when my mind started going, figuring out what we could do with it. In most cases a great beer will combine several hops, although this can be tricky. As I have always said, hops are a bit like people, some get on well and some do not get on so well. In many cases the only way you truly understand is through experimentation of combinations. The alternative that we have had some great success with due to the growing array of fantastic hops available, is to showcase a single hop by brewing a single hop variety beer. Sometimes hops, like people just work better alone.

Hop Regions

Hops, of course, are a natural ingredient in the brewing process and historically this has led to four key hop growing regions, each with their own general characteristics. Of course, prior to the globalisation of the world these would have been the hops available to brewers in these different regions which is why these areas were originally known for certain beer styles. Which just shows how the hops available dictate the style of beer that can be brewed. The regions include:

European Hop Varieties: These would typically be floral, and spicy. Includes many of the German style hops such as Saaz and Tettnang which are used in the fantastic German style Pilsners they are so famous for.

English Hop Varieties: These would be fruity, resinous and spicy. Includes the iconic Challenger and Northdown hops so perfectly suited for malty amber or best bitters the UK was historically so famous for, such as our Business as Usual.

American Hop Varieties: These would be citrusy, herbal and resinous. Great examples would be Mount Hood and Wakatu perfectly suited to American Pale Ales and IPAs which the US craft beer movement have made famous.

Pacific Hop Varieties: These would be fruity, citrusy and floral, such as Nelson Sauvin and Motueka suited to the golden ales, pacific lagers and pale ales of the region.

Today the lines are much more blurred with several new hop varieties grown all over the world. For example, Jester is grown in the UK, although it is very similar to hops grown in the Pacific region in terms of its characteristics and flavour profile. Or Willamette grown in the US but very similar to English hops in terms of flavour and characteristics. There is easy access to a world of hops and we now all brew a huge variety of beer styles, but this helps to explain why certain beer styles have become synonymous with certain regions. When it comes to bittering hops many people have stayed with what they have used before as these lend themselves well to bittering. An example is your Goldings and English hop, which is just a classic bittering hop, which is why it appears in so many wonderful beers.

A Brewer in a Sweet Shop

When it comes to hops, one of the challenges is simply the choice of hops now available. Every brewery will have its own bible of hops, which is literally a huge book of all the current hops available, with all the data on each hop, alpha %, and flavour profile.

To a brewer, it's like being a kid in a sweetshop as they are working through the hop bible to create a recipe for a new beer. Of course, over the years all brewers will have their favourite hops, ones they have brewed with before, combinations they have tried, and of course personal favourites, just like beer drinkers have theirs. The beauty is, as a brewer, there's always an exciting new hop to try out. As we have already touched on when looking at combinations of hops and balancing that in your recipe, the hop's alpha must be considered.

The alpha is a guide to the strength of the hop. So, when you are looking at working with a new hop, you can use this guide to understand the impact this will have on your beer.

My Favourite Hops

Finding my favourite hops is part and parcel of developing so many recipes over the years. I have only been able to do this by working my way through the hop bible, which has been a pleasure. So, I'd like to share some of my favourite hops, although there's so many great ones.

When it comes to great English hops my absolute favourite has to be Northdown, because it changed the way I brew. I had always used Goldings and Fuggles in combination but the introduction of Northdown took this to another level. It gave that little extra on the floral side. Helping to make the beer more sessionable, and it led to the creation of our best selling and highly awarded Business as Usual.

In terms of new world hops it would have to be Citra for me. It's just a remarkable hop, and in combination with Simcoe which is how I used to use it, can really produce some fantastic beers. Although there are no steadfast rules other than the magic balance.

What I have really enjoyed in recent years is the harmonisation of hops and the influence across the globe, doing a full 360. Many American brewers have started to purchase UK Hops, Fuggles and Goldings. America very much led the way during the craft beer revolution. With some iconic breweries and beers starting off with a completely different take on beers, compared to the UK market at the time, so it's great to see it going back the other way. Of course, this would have been heavily influenced by the hops they had available to them in those regions. Naturally leading to the more hop forward beers that are now synonymous with craft beer revolution. Of course, many UK brewers now brew these styles of beers so well. For me though, this is a huge compliment for UK brewers where US brewers have clearly enjoyed UK beers and are now wanting to replicate these beers by using UK hops themselves. I feel the UK brewing industry is just not celebrated enough. Unfortunately, we just don't make many things anymore in the UK. But one thing we do make is great beer, without doubt some of the best in the world!

Make It a Whole Hop

Something many people don't realise is that hops come in three different options. You can purchase hops as whole hops, hop pellets and hop plugs. Without doubt the best proposition and one that we have always used are the whole hops.

When you handle a whole hop, you feel the whole flower in your hand and of course feel the hop resin or oil between your fingers. It is this that retains the fruitier flavours derived from the hop. In recent years this has led to the trend for unfiltered lagers, craft beers and even unfined craft ales. This leads to the bigger fruity flavours that brewers are looking to achieve. It's the loss of the hop resin and oils that takes away these fantastic fruity flavours so prevalent in these high alpha hops.

This is not the case in the hop plugs. The whole hops are crushed into a powder and then pressed together into the desired shape through the pellet mill. This makes the hops easier to handle and saves on transport costs, but it undoubtedly comes at the cost of flavour, as some of the hop oils and resin is left on the pellet mill.

In hop pellets the whole hops are cut into sections and formed into disks. This is not as damaging as the plug process, but it will still reduce the oils and resin retained in the hops. Again, this makes the hops easier to handle and saves on transport costs.

In both cases the larger scale beer factories favour these versions of hops for ease. For me there can only be one winner when it comes to convenience and cost saving verses flavour, which is why it must be whole hops all the way!

It's so easy to get lost in the world of hops, as after all it's just so diverse today. Coming back to our focus of making a great beer from a hop perspective, this in my view is particularly challenging. In some ways, with so many great hops how could you go wrong? But as I touched on earlier, it's about combinations of hops that work well together. I have always believed that a great beer must be one where you can't just have that one pint but want to keep coming back again and again and again. We always say we are in the business of selling the second and third pint. From a purely selfish point of view that means we sell more beer. The drinker is enjoying the beer, and the landlord is also selling the beer by quickly keeping it fresh, so everyone's happy. From a hop point of view this must come from balance. We have all drunk those beers that are so hop heavy, and packed full of super high alpha hops, that after half a pint your pallet has given up the ghost and that second half is hard work, so you're certainly not buying another. So, I think we can all agree a great beer should never be a chore to drink. With careful consideration (more of this in the recipe section) you can produce a beer that is packed full of flavour, and you can thoroughly enjoy a pint or two of it.

It must be something that people will return to time and time again, which you achieve when you have that magic word, BALANCE. So, in most cases you have a good hunch where your absolute beer winners are before it leaves the brewery!

Secret 5:

Yeast

Without Yeast There Is No Alcohol

Simply, without yeast there is no alcohol. Yeast's main job is to convert the sugars in the wort into alcohol and ultimately create beer. This takes around five days depending on the strength of the alcohol in the beer, or ABV, but more on these brew timings later.

Yeast is an often-overlooked element of both what makes a great beer by drinkers and many in the industry alike and one that I have learned has a huge impact on the finished product. Yeast can add real depth and flavour to the beer. You can also enhance the fruity hop flavours depending on the yeasts used. For example, the Californian yeast is designed to enhance fruity flavours. Or even take yeast from another drinks category. We have used a champagne yeast on one beer to add a dry brute taste profile. So, yeast can have a real bearing on the finished taste profile.

Different yeasts also work differently. A traditional ale yeast is top fermenting designed for open fermentation vessels. A lager must use a bottom fermenting lager yeast. As a lager is fermented in an enclosed dual-purpose fermentation vessel, a top fermenting yeast is not suitable. For a lager to be a true lager, it must be allowed to lager or mature in vessel for at least 4–6 weeks. This must be done in an enclosed vessel to keep the beer safe, if of course you allow the lager to lager and mature that is. Unfortunately, the big, mass-produced lagers such as Carling are simply brewed and sent out to trade in just a few days. They skip this key stage as it adds significant costs due to stock holding. The issue is if you do skip this stage a harsher taste profile is prevalent, rather than a smoother more mellow flavour of a true lager such as the iconic Czech Pilsners. I will never forget my tour of Budweiser Budvar, where in huge cellars below the brewery their maturation vessels are housed. As far as the eye can see, vessel after vessel with brewed beer simply lagering or maturing and developing its flavour. This is the reason it needs to be matured in an enclosed vessel, to protect the beer, but it also means you can't crop the yeast from the top. Instead, you take the yeast from the bottom of the vessel, hence the need for a bottom fermenting lager yeast.

I must admit that amidst the flurry of setting up my first brewery, yeast was not something I had initially considered. I was adding a brewery to my real ale pub, The Brunswick Inn, Derby. One of the first ever free houses, where unusually at the time beers were sourced from across the country. Rather than a brewery simply selling their own beers, we sold lots of beer and had great relationships with many of the breweries whose beer we sold. The free house concept is not so unusual now but at that time breweries had their own pubs and sold their own beer, so to have such a selection of beer was a complete novelty. I was a bit of a cask beer nut with 17 hand pulls of beer on every day. This gives you an idea of the amount of beer we sold through, and we put on huge beer festivals, but I had always wanted to brew my own beer.

The Call That Changed My Brewing Journey

I was working on getting the brewery ready when I was fortunate enough to receive a phone call from Stuart Bateman of Batemans Brewery, a good friend and one of our brewery suppliers. At the time, Batemans were one of the most awarded brewers in the industry and the brewer of the iconic XXXB, a former CAMRA Champion Beer of Britain. Batemans are a legacy brewery, now in their fourth generation and one of the oldest regional family brewers, brewing since 1874! Stuart had heard via the grapevine that I was putting in a brewing plant. At the time we sold large quantities of Batemans beer and he simply said, "I wonder if I can be of assistance. Trevor, would you consider using Batemans yeast to brew with?" At that point my first brew was some time off, and I had not considered what yeast to use, but I loved Batemans beers, so the answer had to be yes! Batemans have their own live yeast strain. So, once ready, the yeast was delivered with our weekly beer order. I hadn't realised at the time, but this would set my beers apart from the crowd as it was very unusual for a new brewery to use a live yeast like this, with most using Nottingham dried yeast. Of course, with the level of brewing heritage Batemans had developed their own yeast over many years. This really was a coup and ultimately led to us developing our very own Derby Brewing live yeast strain many years later.

Dried Yeast

At the time as referenced most new brewers simply used Nottingham dried yeast, which many still use to this day. Similar to what you bake bread with for all those home bakers. In the same way, it's a dried yeast that you add water to. Which just like live yeast is then pitched into the beer to begin the fermentation process. You use it once for the brew and then dispose of it and then pitch another batch for the next brew. It's not possible to crop a dried yeast. Cropping the yeast is the process of taking the excess yeast from the top of the fermenter and then using it on subsequent brews. This avoids any need for yeast management or any of the extra work that goes into this, and any associated risk.

Live Yeast

A live yeast on the other hand is in liquid form and needs to be nurtured. It's a living organism after all. As such, between brews the yeast must be kept in refrigerated tubs. So, prior to pitching the yeast or adding it to the fermentation vessel of filled wort, it must be brought out of the fridge to warm up to room temperature, so not to shock it when adding it to the wort. This is the last stage on the brew day prior to the clean down. During the fermentation process the yeast will be cropped and transferred to sterilised containers and refrigerated until it needs to be used again on subsequent brews. On the other hand, dried yeast is always ready to be used by just adding water. Not everyone would have had such a kind offer as the one I received especially in the beginning of their brewing journey. Or be willing to develop their own live yeast strain. Most new brewers use dried yeast as there is a lot less work involved. Today there are some great dried yeasts available for specific beer styles. We have previously used a Californian yeast, which was designed to help bring out the fruity hop flavours in Pale Ales and IPAs, but at the time it was much more limited, so I was delighted to receive the phone call from Batemans.

As I mentioned this later led to us developing our own Derby Brewing Yeast Strain in 2010 with the help of Dominic Flynn, a former head brewer. This is now our registered yeast and is regrown by our Brew Chemist every fifth generation, as exactly the same yeast but brand new, which ensures it is fresh to keep it strong. This avoids the risk of it getting tired, which can lead to it taking too long to ferment the beer out. It also avoids the possibility that it could latch onto a wild yeast strain, which would dramatically change the flavour of the beer. Some brewers have been operating with the same generation for 15 years, but I prefer to rather not take the risk. There's an extra cost associated with growing a new culture every fifth generation, or around every couple of months. Once cultured we must allow the yeast to build, so we would never pitch the fledgling yeast on a stronger 5% plus beer but rather on a lower ABV beer. The stronger the beer, the more work you are asking the yeast to do. Put it this way, you wouldn't go out and run a marathon straight out the bat, would you?

It's essential that once pitched the yeast gets to work quickly, to ensure the fermentation takes place in a timely fashion so not to cause bottlenecks in the brewery. It's also important that the yeast forms its usual protective layer on the top of the beer, which would typically form within 24 hours, reducing the chance of any contaminants entering the beer, which could lead to off flavours.

Yeast's Impact on Flavour

In terms of flavour yeast does have a major bearing on the finished product, as mentioned earlier. In fact, I can always tell when a brewery has used dried Nottingham yeast in terms of the taste profile of the beer. A great example of this would be when recommencing brewing in the pandemic. We were brewing quite infrequently due to reduced demand. To maintain a live yeast, you must brew at least once a week, so we had no option but to use the Nottingham dried yeast on our best-selling beer Business as Usual, instead of our Derby Brewing live yeast that we normally use. The result was a beer that was very different and lacked the malty body that is always there with Business as Usual. Everything else was the same but it shows just what a difference the yeast can make. Our live yeast enhanced the flavours making the dried yeast alternative taste bland in comparison.

This is why we use the Derby Brewing Yeast in all our core beers. We are always striving for the consistency that we believe is crucial to making great beer. As I said, we use a variety of quality dried yeasts from across the world in specials when we are looking for something different, taking the opportunity to experiment. Yeast is now another part of the brewer's armoury to help achieve the flavour profile they are looking for, so it must be considered depending on the beer style.

I often think back to the phone call I received all those years ago, as I may have just ended up blending into the crowd with the usual Nottingham dried yeast. It is unlikely that we would have created our own yeast strain as a result. The pandemic example showed just what an impact that would have had on our beers. So, in reality, would I have won the awards I have and had the success I have enjoyed as a brewer without this? Of course, everyone is always talking about the malt, hops and the recipe that makes great beers but it's quite clear to me that yeast has a major part to play in making great beer!

Secret 6:

Temperature

The Non-Negotiable

In this respect brewing is very similar to cooking. To get the most from your great ingredients there are some fundamental temperatures that must be achieved through the brewing process. If these key temperatures are not achieved you can lose beer, develop off flavours and even stop the fermentation process itself. Meaning you don't convert those sugars to alcohol, so your wort never becomes a beer at all!

Mash Tun

The first, and probably the most fundamental temperature, in the brewing process is your mash temperature. The key here is to ensure the water which has the freshly milled malt mixed in by hand to form a lovely thick porridge is always between 66 and 68 degrees. To maintain this mash temperature, the water which is used later to sparge or sprinkle over the top of the mash should also be 66 to 68 degrees. The reason that this temperature is so critical is, not to get too technical, but at this temperature the starch in the malt begins to melt. In essence you kick start all the sugars in the malt and therefore have the best opportunity to draw these out of the malt flavour into your wort and ultimately your beer. Of course, these are the very sugars that are converted to alcohol. You are literally mashing the malt in the water like a giant cup of tea trying to get the most flavour you can into your beer. This process takes around 75 minutes. As we now know, malt is the foundation of the beer's body. Everything has been about building up this moment.

To maximise the flavour, we have already selected the best malt we can to fit the beer we are trying to create. Finding the balance, we are looking for and sparing no expense in getting the right foundation and body for our beer. We have also freshly milled these malts less than 12 hours before we get the mash in, but all of this will be wasted if this one temperature is not accurate. When you get it right, though, there's nothing like that beautiful malty smell in the air on a chilly winter's morning, safe in the knowledge that you have temps right and you are getting all of that straight into your beer.

There really is no ifs, buts, or maybes. This temp must be right. I literally had this drilled into me by Chris Marchbanks, the brewing consultant that taught me how to brew from my brewhouse at the Brunswick. He taught me by brewing with me day after day until he was happy that I was ready to brew on my own. In fact, he stayed far longer than I had paid him for and refused to take any more money. He really was a great guy. Sadly, he's no longer with us but I can honestly say I couldn't have been a brewer without him and his influence. He was so committed to making me a brewer, and he did it by simply becoming one of the team. So, I really did learn alongside him. He simply wouldn't leave until he was 100% happy that I could do it. Never mind everything else I have achieved over the years, none of this would have been possible without Chris.

If you don't get your mash temp right, you simply can't get your mash in. As without the right temperature you simply won't get all that flavour from those hand selected malts into your beer. It will remain in spent malt and it will also reduce your extract, or the amount of beer you end up with. The density of the beer would be reduced. The denser it is, the higher the concentration or strength of beer that will be produced. So, to bring the alcoholic volume down to the level you are looking for would mean you need to add water to the wort, a process known as watering back. So, the lower the density the less beer you will end up with and the higher the density, the more beer you will have. So not getting enough from your malt reduces both flavour and hurts you commercially as you have less beer to sell from the same ingredient cost.

If you don't get this right, then the spent malt is still full of the flavour that should have been in your beer. After being hand dug out of the Mash Tun by shovel the spent malt heads to a local farm and is used as pig feed, so those pigs are enjoying your costly mistake. You don't mind digging out the spent grain, always hot and heavy work, if you know you have all the flavour it must give. Thankfully, I have never missed hitting the right temps, so I quite enjoy the dig out. I have always described it as a workout in a sauna. You never know, maybe it was the inspiration for hot yoga.

The Boil

The next temperature is of course the boil in the copper. Once you have got your mash in, you transfer the wort into the copper which is essentially a giant kettle to boil up all the ingredients. Once the coils in the copper are covered, it's the big switch on and the copper starts to build the wort temperature up from 66–67 degrees to 100 degrees. Once the boil has been achieved, the bittering hops will be added, and there's a rolling boil for 75 minutes. Which is, essentially, the cooking process. The aroma hops are added 20 minutes before the rolling boil is completed. The wort is then allowed to rest for 30 minutes, which allows all the solids in the wort to settle and drop down below the thimble in the copper—this is mainly spent hops. This process helps to improve the clarity of your beer and helps the flavour of the beer stabilise. If they remained in the beer the flavour would continue to evolve, increasing bitterness levels over time.

Cooling the Wort for Fermentation

At this point in the brew the wort will be a high eighty degrees, which becomes a problem as the wort is then transferred to the fermentation vessel. Yeast will be added, ready for the magic to happen, and those sugars will be converted into alcohol, turning the wort into beer. The issue is that yeast can't survive at these temperatures. For fermentation to work effectively it must be at 18 to 20 degrees. This is when the paraflow is used to bring the temperature down to these levels. I like to explain a paraflow as a backwards radiator, where the hot beer is passed through it directly alongside coils of cold water. The water never comes into direct contact with the wort, but the close proximity of the pipework brings the temperature down. The temperature of the water and speed at which the wort is passed through the paraflow controls how much the temperature drops. So, in the winter this run off process is much quicker but in the height of summer this takes longer, as the incoming tap water temperature is higher. So, the wort must be passed through the paraflow more slowly to drop the required amount. The process however takes as long as it takes. In fact, my record was one scorching summer's day when I spent 15 hours on the brew day from start to finish. Much of that down to the runoff length. Afterwards it's the clean, as you can't go home until the brewery is spotless just like you found it.

If this maximum 20 degrees hasn't been achieved, then quite simply there will be slow, or no fermentation. Initially this will leave the beer unprotected as the active yeast quickly forms a layer on top of the open fermentation vessel. So, in addition to converting those sugars into alcohol, it protects the beer and anything getting into the beer that shouldn't. If the beer is not fermented out in a timely fashion this can lead to off flavours, create bottlenecks in the production process and in extreme cases it will mean that you have no beer at all, as without alcohol there is of course no beer.

One brew day at the Brunswick, I was approaching the end of my brew, and it was time for collection and to crucially get the wort down to 18 to 20 degrees. Unfortunately, my subversive pump had other ideas and died. Meaning I was unable to draw up the water from the well to cool the beer through the paraflow. I knew the wort could not be transferred at the high temp it was at, as the yeast would not survive. Something I had never encountered before. Thankfully, after my time working with Chris I never felt on my own. I have always found brewing to be such a fantastic welcoming industry. Whether that be like-minded brewers looking to help each other by lending ingredients if you are caught short on a delivery, or in this case when it comes to advice.

Bruce to the Rescue

For me, Bruce Wilkinson of Burton Bridge has always been there to help. Bruce followed a different route to becoming a multi-award-winning brewer. He was a good friend and thankfully one that was always on hand when I came across something, just like this, that was out of the ordinary. Bruce, unlike me, had all his brewing bits of paper, something he would always remind me of when I found myself stuck. So, he would take the piss but always give me the answer. Thankfully Bruce knew what to do. He simply said leave the wort in copper overnight and then collect once your replacement pump is fitted in the morning. The issue was the wort was sat on the hops all night, increasing the bitterness well beyond normal levels. He said, "Keep sampling the wort as you collect, as at some point the bitterness is going to be so high it will pin your ears back and the beer will become undrinkable." He predicted I'd lose 50% of the brew and he was bang on, as always. Showing just how essential the runoff temperature is and, of course, knowing the right people.

Fermentation

It's also just as important to maintain the 18-to-20-degree temperature during the fermentation process. The process of fermentation also creates heat, hence why fermentation vessels must be temperature controlled. Commercial FVs have automatic temperature controls, kicking in and maintaining a set temperature just like your central heating at home. They can even text you if there is a problem. The final temperature change in the fermentation process, once the beer has fermented out to the desired ABV, is when the FV is put onto cool, normally to around 5 degrees. This kills off the yeast and stops it continuing the process. It also makes it easy to transfer the beer around the brewery, as the cold temperature makes the beer less lively, reducing wastage.

Fill Those Casks

The 5-degree beer is then transferred to the raking tanks which are housed in our cold store and are maintained at the temperature of a pub cellar, being 12 degrees. The beer remains in the raking tanks for 24 hours. The beer is then filled into casks and again stored in the cold store, in cask until delivery. Raking tanks helps improve the beer clarity. Although many brewers fill casks directly from the FV, we add this extra step. By doing this, more of the yeast is removed from the cask. By transferring into the raking tanks and filling the casks from there, more of the yeast is removed as during those 24 hours it settles below the thimble. Meaning the beer will clear more quickly in cask and be better behaved as it ages. The beer will be less likely to be a beer bomb in someone's cellar.

Making Life Easy for Pubs

I believe that to be a great brewer it's important to look after the people that look after and care for your beer once it's left the brewery. The people who look after the beer in the cellar of the pub where it is going to be sold. Beer is a live product so it must be properly cared for. It's our job as brewers to make that process as easy as possible. Pub owners want a tasty beer that will clear quickly and behave, meaning the beer will drop clear quickly. If that's how its intended to be served that is. Also, that it's not excessively lively, meaning you are not going to be wearing the beer or have it end up all over the cellar floor, so they can get the beer onto the bar and for sale as quickly as possible. From a brewer's perspective if your beer doesn't clear or ends up on the cellar ceiling, this will just upset customers and lead to you having to replace, or in the worst case, refund the beer. In fact, there was once a lovely beer called Timothy Taylors Porter which was probably the biggest beer bomb I have ever come across. Literally every time you opened one it would fire beer out at you—the classic beer shower. In the end it was discontinued due to these issues. I guess Timothy Taylor got fed up with the complaints and having to give beer away. They never like to do that, being from Yorkshire!

So, as you can see there are not many key temperature moments in the brewing process. For me there's no doubt that if you don't get your temperatures right you can't brew a great beer or any beer at all for that matter!

Secret 7:

Time

Without Consistency There Can't Be Great Beer

As we have now established, consistency and process are fundamental to brewing great beer. Of course, timings form a crucial part of this, and are repeated time after time. To help demonstrate this consistent process I am going to walk you through the process. Starting on your prep day, the crucial day before the big day, through the fermentation, barrelling and even all the way to the finished beer we all enjoy over the bar.

Prep Day

Prep day, the key here is to make sure that everything is ready for you to come in on the brew day and start brewing. That means malt is milled and in place and, crucially, your water is ready and at temperature for your mash. In terms of malt there are two different options. You can purchase ready milled malt, as most brewers of our size would. As detailed however, much like a coffee bean, the longer you leave the malt after milling before you brew with it, the less flavour you will extract from the malt. It is not uncommon for brewers to brew with pre-milled malt that has been milled three weeks or more prior to brewing.

For me, as soon as I wanted to brew, I knew I had to have a mill, as there seemed little point in buying the most expensive malt in the world and not getting the maximum flavour possible from it.

Of course, prior to milling the malt you would need to weigh out the recipe, typically this would include several full 25kg bags. Plus, the combination of the malts that make up the lower percentage of your grist, all weighed to the kilogram, depending on your recipe. Which would all be milled in with the full bags, ready to go into the mash the following day.

This milling process would usually take between four and five hours for our 15-barrel plant, with the malt being milled no longer than 12 hours prior to getting the mash in. Of course, milling your own malt creates a whole lot more cleaning, as you look like a ghost by the end of it. Covered top to toe in white malt dust, which gets all over the brewery. If you can imagine someone has completely covered you in flour, then you get the picture. However, to get the maximum flavour in your beer it's totally worth it and has always been a non-negotiable for me!

While you're milling you would also be bringing your water to temperature by heating it up in your copper. You would heat this above the required 66–68 degrees to allow for temperature drop off. Some of the water would then be transferred into your hot liquor tanks, ready for sparging the mash the following day. The hot liquor tanks are insulated and can be heated via electric heaters if required. The water which will be used to mash with will remain in the copper ready to be transferred on the brew day itself.

So that's your prep day. Your malt is milled, and your water is where it needs to be and as close to temperature as possible.

Another Day of Beer

On brew day, I'd bounce into the brewery full of beans for another day of beer! First job would be to turn on the copper to increase the temperature of the water that was prepared yesterday, generally only by a few degrees to get it back up to the magic 66–68 degrees. As you would likely have lost some temperature overnight. This would take half an hour to three quarters of an hour.

Getting the Mash In

At which point you transfer the water from the copper, into your Mash Tun. This is the first stage of getting the Mash Tun prepared, with the water always to the same consistent level on the Mash Tun.

Then to start getting your mash in, its literally a case of you grabbing the paddle and hand turning the freshly milled malt into your water as it drops down from the mill above the Mash Tun. Whilst you're mixing it in you are controlling the speed, to ensure the malt is evenly mixed. Mix until you have formed a nice thick porridge but, crucially, without any lumps of unmixed malt. This would usually take 30–45 minutes.

You would then allow the mixture to rest for around 75 minutes. Periodically, sparging or sprinkling water from your hot liquor tanks that you prepared the day before over the top to keep it moist. At this point you are infusing the lovely malt flavours into your water which will of course form the body of your wort and then beer.

Run Off

The next stage would be your run off, the process of transferring all the lovely malt infused water from your Mash Tun into your copper to start the boil. The liquid, now known as wort, is transferred via the large stainless-steel bath known as the underback. You open the valve on the Mash Tun and fill the bath via a stainless pipe, almost like opening the tap on your bath at home.

To get the most flavour as possible into your wort you continue to sparge or sprinkle water over the top of the malt, but you increase the quantity of water. It usually takes around five full underbacks or baths, which are transferred from the Mash Tun and into the copper for the boil.

The key here is to maintain a layer of water on top of the malt of no more than a couple of centimetres, being careful not to add too much as the weight of the water will force the malt down, blocking the Mash Tun pipe and creating what is called a set mash. Meaning the pipe or tap that transfers the wort into the underback becomes blocked. This happens to everyone at some point and if you're lucky it won't be 100% blocked. In the case of a full blockage, you must blast the wort back into the Mash Tun to force the malt backup and clear the blockage. I can tell you it's a hell of a game! Usually, you are looking at two hours for a normal run off but you can add at least another hour for the dreaded set mash.

The Roar of the Copper

Once the coils of the copper are covered it's the big copper switch on, as it roars into life. This allows you to start heating up the wort as you fill up the copper, saving some time bringing the wort to a boil. As you are transferring the wort you should carry out checks on the gravity. If its higher than you are going for, you should add water, this is known as liquoring back prior to the boil. This is crucial to get the gravity to the level of your recipe and the ABV correct, as ultimately those sugars are converted into alcohol. You would allow 75 minutes for a rolling boil with the bittering hops added shortly after rolling boil is achieved, then adding your aroma hops 10 minutes before the end.

Once boiled, as you can imagine, you will have wort and hops all over the place in the copper, so it's important to allow the wort to rest for 30 minutes. At this point the hops continue to infuse, mainly the aroma hops which have only just been added. It also allows the hops to settle to the bottom of the copper, below the thimble. Crucially removing them from the wort, as you would not want to transfer those hops beyond the copper.

The Consistent Dry Hop

When the wort has been allowed to rest it's time to start the transfer of the wort into the fermentation vessel, via the underback. Or if it's part of the recipe, it's also the time for what I have referred to as the consistent dry hop. All the wort passes through the hop basket into the underback. The hop basket is a round stainless-steel bucket with a mesh bottom. It is attached to the transfer pipe from the copper and housed in the middle of the underback or stainless-steel bath. This hop basket should be filled with the desired dry hop. The bath should be filled with wort, which should then be left to infuse in this first full bath of wort for 20 minutes. Literally soaking up all that hoppy goodness from your aroma hop. All the remaining wort should also pass through those same hops, to ensure a consistent dry hop throughout the wort.

Collection

Once the initial soak has taken place you should then start the collection process, passing the hot wort through the paraflow to reduce the temperature of the wort. Oxygen is also added as it's transferred into the fermentation vessel. This is called Oxygenating. This would usually take a couple of hours but can take longer during the warm summer months when the incoming water temperature is higher. Once there is a decent amount of wort in the fermentation vessel the chosen yeast would be pitched into the vessel by adding some of the wort into the bucket containing the weighed-out yeast to help kick start the process before pouring the yeast into the vessel.

Now that the brew itself is completed, and the beer is safely in the vessel, it's the clean down—which is usually a couple of hours. Some brewers leave the brewery at this point, this is just like leaving the dishes in the sink all night, but on a huge scale. It is just going to increase the workload of the clean when they come to it, as its dried on. I have always believed it isn't good practice. Not to mention, it drives my OCD cleaning crazy! There's also the risk that it can get into the atmosphere. So after I have cleaned everything down, the entire brewery is flushed with peracetic acid so its left spick and span and ready for the next brew!

When the Magic Happens

The yeast is now doing its thing, the magic is happening as those sugars are converted into alcohol. This usually takes five days or so, depending on the strength of the beer. As its less work for the yeast to convert less sugar to alcohol, the lower ABV or strength beers can be a little faster and vice versa for the stronger beers taking longer.

Often temperature also plays a role here, as on a very cold winters night the yeast may not kick in and start the fermentation process. I have even had cases where I have waited a couple of days and it's not kicked in. At this point, there is no other option than to grab the paddle you use to mash in with and literally bash the yeast over the head to wake it up. It's called rousing the yeast. You stir the wort, getting as much air into it as possible, almost in a whisk motion. With the aim of adding oxygen to wort to help the yeast and encourage it to kick into life, letting it know there's a job to be done! Obviously, this would increase your fermentation time. At this point you should continue to test for gravity or strength of the beer as it ferments out to the desired ABV.

Dry Hop in FV

It would be at this point you could add the dry hop in vessel. So, you are adding a further dry hop to the beer during the fermentation process. Dry hopping in FV would usually only be added on day two or three of the fermentation, once it's usually underway. As a result, and to allow the hops enough time to infuse into your beer, it will increase your time in the vessel by a couple of days depending on the desired flavour profile. With typical dry hopping in vessel being 2–4 days.

Raking and Filling Those Casks

The final stage for the beer at the brewery is transferring the now fermented beer from the FV into the raking tanks. This process will further remove yeast from the beer as its left in the FV and, of course, any hops used for dry hopping.

Many brewers fill the casks directly from the FV however we transfer the beer to raking tanks, in our cold store. This is where its allowed 24 hours to settle before raking or filling the casks. This further removes yeast and improves the clarity of the beer.

Fining the Beer

The final stage is of course delivering the beer to the pub or venue it's going to be enjoyed in. To prepare the beer for delivery we would at this stage add finings to the beer. If it's a beer designed to be clear that is. Of course, there is a growing trend for unfined beers or hazy beers. This is normally for hop forward beers with higher alpha fruity hops, as it leaves more of the hop resin in the beer, meaning you are enjoying more of the fruity hop flavours. It really depends on your preference but when it comes to traditional style malty beers, brewed with lower alpha and less fruity hops, they are always served crystal clear, as there would be no benefit to leaving the beer unfined. The finings is a solution that works by grabbing all the sediment or yeast in the beer and dragging it to the bottom of the barrel, below the tap. Meaning you are left with perfectly crystal clear or shiny beer. When a barrel goes or is empty, you have reached the sediment at the bottom and the beer becomes cloudy, which is when the barrel should be changed. We are very passionate that our beers, when intended, are served perfectly clear. In fact, I couldn't resist naming one of my first beers from Derby Brewing Shiny Beer and, of course, it was!

It is for this reason that we prefer to store our beer raw in the cold store. We do this as the finings are most effective the first few times they are used. So, if you add finings when barrelling the beer from the raking tanks the finings will, by their nature, be disturbed more times prior to being delivered to the pub. Meaning when you really want it to work it's going to be less effective. Of course, the larger mass-produced brewers add finings when the beer is barrelled meaning they can put less beer in the cask, saving money but potentially meaning the beer might not shine in the glass.

Delivery and the Perfect Pint

So, once we receive an order, we open the beer and add finings just prior to delivery to the pub.

Of course, looking after the beer properly once it's been delivered to the pub is equally important. Cask beer is, after all, a live product so needs to be cared for; something I have taken great pride in for many years and across all our pubs.

First the beer is given a good roll to properly disturb the beer and allow the finings to mix evenly prior to putting it onto stillage in the cellar. This allows the finings to grab any yeast in the beer, dragging it below the tap. This is called allowing the beer to settle. It is generally left around 12 hours. The cask is then tapped and left for a further 24 hours when it will drop crystal clear, if that's how it's intended. With all the sediment below the tap and clear beer above. At this point, it's simply a job of connecting it up to a cleaned line and pulling it through ready to serve and enjoy as it goes over the bar.

So that completes the beer's journey, from prep day to finally being served as the perfect pint to the customer. The key in timings as you can see is simply consistency. Allowing the process to be followed and ample time given to each stage, to get the best out of your ingredients. Although beers evolve, the key is always only to change one thing at a time. Every other part of the process from recipe, timings, temperatures and more must remain the same apart from the one element you are looking to tweak. So, without consistent timings you simply can't have consistency and therefore you can't have a great beer that can be enjoyed time and time again.

Secret 8:

Recipe

Finding the Balance

Any great beer, unsurprisingly, is the combination of all the best ingredients that go into the beer and, in my view, finding the balance within that to allow those incredible ingredients to shine in harmony together! I have thought long and hard about how best to share what makes a great recipe, but I think the best way is to talk through the process I have followed when creating a new beer over the years. Combined with the example recipes included to see what the finished article looks like. This is the best way to guide you through it.

The Foundation of Your Beer

The first consideration must be your base malt. This forms the basis of the body of your beer and it's here that, in my view, you really can't compromise. As detailed in the malt section, for me there is one base malt that stands above all others—Maris Otter, available in both low colour and as it comes. Without question this is the best place to start if you're looking to create a beer with body across all beer styles, although you can switch to, or combine this with a lager malt or Czech lager malt when brewing lagers.

Choose Your Beer Style

As the base is mainly a constant the next consideration is always the beer style you are looking for in terms of your grist of malts that form your mash. So, are you looking for a pale, amber, ruby, or dark beer, for example. Obviously, there are many variations in between these, as we know pales can go from pale straw through to deep golden but generally it's like a funnel. You start light and work your way down from there. The colour of your beer will dictate the malts you want to use but it's also important to consider how you achieve the body of the beer, as a thin beer can never be a great beer.

Percentages of the Grist

Before I start on the separate styles, it's important to explain percentages of the grist, as its commonly referenced in malt recipes. The key here is that it is always percentages of your total grist. You will see this on recipes and referred to by brewers. The percentage is quite simply the percentage of your total grist or malt, in terms of the amount of KG of one malt as a proportion of the total KG of malt used in the recipe. So, the lower the percentage the less KG and less proportion of the total recipe. Hence why certain malts must be kept lower as a percentage to avoid the colour of the beer, or those malts, to dominate the recipe too much.

Pale Beers

I'll work through these from pale, to amber, through to dark beers. In terms of pale ales, the options you have to achieve body are more restricted than an amber or dark beer but there are tricks you can use here to still achieve body without impacting on the colour of the finished beer.

The key is always the percentages used by adding low colour crystal to the grist, for example, but using a very, very low percentage—as little as 2% of the total mash will increase body without impacting on colour or going beyond the pale you are aiming for. Another way to improve the body is the addition of torrified wheat, again on a very low percentage of the grist, as this can add a slight claw to the taste. These couple of tricks will help make your pales stand out in terms of the body of the beers.

These tricks of the trade will also help to add body to the lower ABV beers, as the stronger the beer the more malt is required in the recipe, but also, crucially, the higher the density of the beer. So, I have always believed it is easy to add body to big strong beers with ABV in excess of 5% but to create body down at 3.4% is always the test of a great brewer and recipe.

Amber Beers

Amber beers, there are more options now open to us for building the malty characteristics and body, as a great malty beer should be like a warm hug on a cold day. The way I have always looked to achieve this, and the perfect amber colour, is a combination of crystal malts. So, the crystal malt combined with the type 200 and the type 400 but being careful to keep the percentages down when it comes to the crystal type 400 malt. As otherwise it can go too far along the colour spectrum and away from what you are looking for. The great thing is these crystal malts enjoy life together and can work well in combination. It's just getting the balance right, which is what a great recipe is all about.

Red Ales

Next along the spectrum are the ruby and red ales. These are about using your base of crystals with a little bit more room to play with in terms of the percentage of type 400 combined with chocolate malt. Although, again, you must be careful with your percentages here, to not go too far. I have also found a great trick when trying to bring out that lovely red hews. That perfect tinge of red when you hold the beer up to the light, is the addition of brown malt but at just 2% of the grist.

Dark Beers

Dark beers such as porters, stouts and, of course, the black IPAs, in terms of malt, the world really is your oyster. This is where the fun really begins. It's unbelievable putting your nose over the Mash Tun when you are getting a mash in for a dark beer. Well, it is in our case, as we really go to town with twelve different malt varieties, as there's nothing more disappointing than a thin dark beer that lacks body.

So, in addition to your crystal malts this is when the roast malts come to play, chocolate, black and roast barley. Although it's still important to have balance to your grist. You can use chocolate and black at reasonable levels but as mentioned in the malt chapter, roasted barley is almost a trap. It's the perfect colour you are going for but too much and it will dominate and leave your beer with an unpleasant aftertaste. The other thing to look out for is too much black, as this can give the beer a burnt tasting note, not the tawny, toffee and chocolate flavours we all look for in a dark beer. So even though you have so many more options open to you in dark beers, it's still about getting the blend right. Combining the right malts to the right percentages to get those flavours you're looking for.

Alcohol Content of Your Beer

The final element you must decide on when it comes to your grist or malt is the alcoholic strength of the beer you are looking to produce. As this can impact on the quantity of malt used. For example, we would increase the malt to maximise the beer we produce as naturally the stronger beers will result in a reduced yield or amount of beer created. The increase in malt can help to offset this.

Hops Hops Hops

Your next decision in the foundations of your recipe, now that you have decided upon the style of beer you're brewing, ABV and the malt for your grist, is the hops.

Firstly, your bittering hops followed by your aroma hops. The hops used here will vary depending on if you are creating a pale or a darker beer. For example, it has become the practice to combine three bittering hops in darker beers, completely unheard-of years ago but quite common now. When it comes to your bittering hops, you're looking at different characteristics to your aroma hop. As many of the more subtle fruity elements of the hop will fall away during the boil and you get left with distinct characteristics namely the bitter flavours. Which is why it's important to avoid too higher alpha content hops, as this will leave the unpalatable and far too bitter characteristics—one of those beers where its hard work to drink the second half of the pint. This is why the more expensive high alpha fruity hops are rarely used for bittering, as it would simply be a waste and potentially make the beers less drinkable.

Applying this to a pale ale, the first question is if you are looking for a smoother finish, easy drinking English style pale ale or a pale with a big fruity hit such as an APA where you are looking for those fruity and citrusy hops to come through. In this case it's important to have a grist that can balance off against those hop characteristics and importantly to not get too high on the bittering alpha content. As this will have the opposite effect, completely dominating the beer so that your taste buds just can't cope with a second pint. Although it's rare to produce hop forward amber beers, when it comes to brown ales, red and black IPAs, this is where you can push the boundaries a little more. Especially as the increased body of the grist allows you to balance off some of the higher alpha hops.

Next up is amber beers. Here you're looking to add what I like to call hop body to bolster the malty grist body. This can be done quite easily but it's about utilising those rock steady hops, the likes of Fuggles, Goldings, and Northdown as your bittering hops. These three just work so well together. The three amigos, all a similar mid-level alpha. You can leave it there or you can up the alpha level on the aroma hops, as there's room depending on the taste profile you are after. Some would argue using anything more than a low-level alpha for bittering is wasteful, but I feel sticking rigidly to this restricts your end product. Sometimes you get out what you put in, so you must invest in the ingredients. Without a doubt these solid UK hops add to the body of the beer, the reason why they were traditionally so widely used in Best Bitters.

The next element to consider is not just the hops used, alpha contents, and the balance of those against the grist, but the quantity of hops used. For example, Citra, one of my favourite hops is high in alpha, a perfect aroma hop but due to the alpha content it has potential to dominate the beer. Losing key elements such as the body and malty content of the beer, here its key to control the quantity of hops used. Using it to a lesser degree means you can still enjoy the characterises of this great hop without it dominating and making the beer unbalanced. There is, of course, a market for these very hop heavy beers. Their fans are called hop heads but you're unlikely to sell the second and third pint of this style of beer. So, if very few people go back for a second pint it's never likely to be a classic. I always think if you stay for two even though you came for one, that's when you know you've got a winner!

Yeast

So now we have a beer style, ABV, and hops, it's important to consider the yeast, as touching on different yeasts brings the best out of certain recipes. For example, if this a fruity pale, then a Californian yeast might be a perfect fit, to maximise those fruity taste profiles. If you have a house live yeast then this will fit with most beer styles but if you're brewing a lager in an enclosed FV then you must use a bottom fermenting lager yeast, as it's designed to work in these vessels and more suited to the style of beer.

Balance Balance Balance

For me, great beers are rarely your beer extremes, they find balance. Whether that's one of the most awarded beers like Timothy Taylor landlord, a drinkable flavoursome classic English pale ale, or Oakham Citra where they have used a fantastic high alpha hop but at quantities that mean the beer remains balanced. It just further demonstrates why the most-used word when it comes to recipe is always going to be balance. This allows all the elements of the recipe you have so carefully crafted to be enjoyed in the finished beer, not simply one winning out above all others. That is for me what makes a great recipe, and with the right ingredients a great beer!

80

Conclusion

The Podium

There you have it, the eight secrets that we believe make a great beer. Of course, all of these are crucial to making a beer you can be proud of and people will genuinely enjoy drinking, but this wouldn't be a conclusion without us reaching a feel for what are the fundamental non-negotiables in a great pint. I think the best way is to create our very own podium moment, to see what the big three are, so here comes our top three secrets.

There is one standout above all else. Without a shadow of a doubt, it must be cleanliness. It might sound boring but without cleanliness you simply can't make beer that anyone's likely to even attempt to drink, never mind enjoy! I simply can't stress enough how important it is. My old motto was always when you think it's clean, clean it again, just in case. Which is exactly why I spent a lot of time cleaning vessels and clambering into all sorts of corners of the brewhouse to make sure my stainless steel glistened.

When it comes to the second element, I'm going to cheat a tad if that's allowed, as I feel there needs to be a joint second place, combining two of the key ingredients, malt and hops. For different reasons, these are the fundamental ingredients that go into making your beer and the bedrock of your recipe, so are essential to making a great beer. Ultimately, it's not rocket science but just like cooking—you get out what you put in. Of course, you can have a great recipe but with substandard ingredients, it will be lacking and never become the beer it was destined to be.

So first of all, malt. I think we have established that, without doubt, it simply has to be Maris Otter malt for me. It's the most sure-fire way to produce a beer you know people will enjoy. In fact, I can tell immediately if a beer is brewed with Maris Otter or not—body, flavour balance all rolled into one, the perfect foundation of your beer.

When it comes to hops there are just so many combinations out there but if this is you trying to make your signature beer then there's just no substitute for using hops that you're happy using. Hops you know combine and play well together but of course fit the style of beer you're trying to brew. Not only that, but, as referenced, I can't stress this enough, use whole hops not pellets or plugs, as they are without doubt a better proposition. Unlike the alternatives they have not been cut, pressed, or crushed together. Although this makes the hops easier to use and less messy to weigh out, you lose essential elements of the hops. The hop resin or oil is lost to a varying extent with the alternatives. It's this hop resin that contains so many of the elements of hop flavour you have paid for. This is especially important in more fruity hops. In fact, it's why the trend for unfiltered lagers, craft beers and even unfined craft ales has developed as more of this is retained, leading to those big fruity flavours that are so popular. Those processes can remove the hop oil or resin and it has a huge impact. So, embrace the mess and use those whole hops for maximum flavour. Just be sure to clean it up afterwards.

Finally, its temperature. Without those crucial temperatures you can't get the maximum flavours from the finest malt on the planet and those whole hops! Not to mention, without it, the beer can't be cooked in the first place, fermentation can't take place, and the beer can't remain alive whilst in cask and served to the customer at the optimum temperature to be enjoyed.

So, in the brew process it's all about using the best ingredients you can, combinations of ingredients you know work, and brewing the beer by hitting the non-negotiable temperatures of the brew to pull the absolute most from those ingredients. Of course, if you put those through a brewery without the cleanliness standards required, you will never produce a consistent beer and can have all kinds of off flavours. If it ever even makes it to the bar. Which is why for me, those have to be the top three, with cleanliness taking the top spot, ingredients the runner up, and temperature completing the podium.

I have really enjoyed writing this book with Paul. We really wanted to create a beer book that would bring beer to life in a fun and entertaining way. Cutting back from the science and not over complicating it. Trying to make it simple for people who just love chatting beer as there was really nothing out there doing that. I think I'm a real testament to that in terms of my career. There are, of course, many ways to learn how to brew beer and many different types of brewers out there but for me I wasn't from a science background. I was a landlord who loved beer and had a passion and desire to brew my own beer. Emphasising that it really doesn't have to be over complicated.

The way I see it, when you have something that needs doing you go to the person with the knowledge. So, you need a new plug socket you go to an electrician or a new tap for the garden, you go to a plumber. I knew I wanted to brew beer from a few months of being behind the bar. I just thought if this is what I want to do, then I want to do the whole process, brew the beer, nurture it all the way through to serving a beer over the bar that makes people smile! So, it was common sense to me that I needed a brewing consultant alongside me. Learning in the brewhouse as you go but under expert tuition. It was the best decision I ever made as I can say that hand on heart every single pint that I have created throughout the years has given me great enjoyment. And me, being me, I wouldn't have had that if I had ended up making big mistakes in the early days. Which doesn't happen with someone by your side who knows exactly what to do. It took the hit and miss, as I call it, out of brewing beer. So, from day one I was brewing beer that people were enjoying.

I guess in many ways my brewing consultant experience was a modern-day brewing apprentice, with a bit less getting the teas in. Funnily enough, we have had several apprentices over the years, working alongside me and our other experienced brewers, just like I did all those years ago. They have learnt by doing, in the brewhouse, from people who have been there and done it all before. Personally, it gives me great pleasure to pass on what I know to someone else. In fact, our head brewer at Derby Brewing, Andy Marshall, started at the bottom and learned with us to become an award-winning brewer in his own right. For me, I just love the idea of producing another brewer on the planet.

It's the best demonstration of why we wanted to write this book, that brewing doesn't have to be complicated and you don't need to have degrees in chemistry that many of the other beer books on the market would make you think. In reality the process of brewing is relatively straightforward itself, the skill comes in creating the recipe of course.

We just wanted to share what makes great beer in the simplest way possible. So, people could understand it. So, people who enjoy drinking beer can hopefully take great pleasure from reading about how it's produced, just like they do when they join us for a brewery tour. Maybe even a few people might read the book and think, fingers crossed, it's a bit of me turning their passion for beer into a profession. If that's the case, then my advice is by all means to go and brew beer. Either for yourself, or if you can learn alongside someone else with the knowledge as it saves a lot of time and guess work in the early days. Remember though, that you will always be learning, your beers will never be static. In my view, you evolve your beers over time. The feeling of being able to put a pint of beer you have created over the bar, and it puts smiles on faces, honestly there's no better feeling than that... Well, maybe Derby County winning the league championship twice, but it comes close!

The process of brewing beer may sound a little daunting and drawn out, but I can honestly say once you have done it a few times in real life, it's actually the most natural way of spending the day, with a fantastic outcome. I have brewed thousands of times, often the same beer time and time again, like our best-selling Business as Usual. I just love the process. It's different on a beer you always brew. It's knowing the pleasure that beer will bring to people who drink it, day in and day out. Then there's a completely different feeling you get when you're creating something completely new. It's another level of excitement seeing how it will turn out as you have not had the chance to taste the finished article, but you still get a tremendous satisfaction in repeating your successes of the past.

With all my years in beer its clear to me that there is one other key element that is essential to make a great beer. It's certainly one that I have seen time and time again, when I have spent time with those in the industry, worked alongside them and, of course, talked beer to anyone that will lend an ear. That is quite simply passion for beer! It's what gets you up at silly o'clock with a spring in your step because it's a beer day. It's what drives you to make the best beer you can. I think, like most things, if you don't have that passion then you will taste it in the glass. I don't think there are many brewers of the iconic and truly great beers across the world that don't have a genuine passion and excitement about beer. I have always said it's not just a job, it's a way of life.

Example Recipes

Straight From the Brewhouse

When we were planning the book, we felt it was important to include some example recipes of key beer styles. So, we have decided to include the following beer styles to give a good cross section of recipes. The recipes are based on a 10 brewers barrel recipe or 1640 litres.

Recipes included:

- English Pale Ale

- American Pale Ale

- English IPA

- American Golden Ale

- Single Hop IPA

- Best Bitter

- Red Ale

- Dark Beer

We have selected this range of beers as we felt these cover a range of malts in the grist, showing how body is achieved across a range of colour profiles, some traditional style beers, and more hop forward beers to help demonstrate the balance we have referenced throughout the book when talking through the individual ingredients and recipe section.

English Pale Ale 4% ABV

A classic light sessionable light pale ale.

Grist		
Malt	**%**	**KG**
Finest Maris Otter® Ale Malt	91	262.18
Torrefied Wheat	9	27.62

Salts and Copper Finings	
Item	**Grams**
DWB	1250

Hops		
Hop	**Grams**	**Stage**
Admiral	1100	Kettle
Goldings	1500	Kettle
Mount Hood	750	Kettle
Mount Hood	1500	Hop Basket

American Pale Ale 4.5%

Combination of solid body and fruity citrusy flavours.

Grist		
Malt	**%**	**KG**
Finest Maris Otter® Ale Malt	95	313.13
Cara Gold Malt	5	18.71

Salts and Copper Finings	
Item	**Grams**
DWB	1250
Copper Finings	14 tabs

Hops		
Hop	**Grams**	**Stage**
Admiral	1000	Kettle
Halletau Blanc	815	Mid Boil
Halletau Blanc	600	Aroma
Citra	500	Hop Basket

English IPA 5.2%

Golden body combined in this sessionable IPA.

Grist		
Malt	**%**	**KG**
Finest Maris Otter® Ale Malt	90	332.32
Wheat Malt	7.2	26.14
Rye Malt	2.8	9.86

Salts and Copper Finings	
Item	**Grams**
DWB	1250

Hops		
Hop	**Grams**	**Stage**
Eagle	1000	Kettle
Brewers Gold	1000	Kettle
Brewers Gold	600	Aroma
Goldings	500	Aroma

American Golden Ale 5.6%

Golden balanced hoppy ale.

Grist		
Malt	**%**	**KG**
Finest Maris Otter® Ale Malt	90	383.08
Torrified Wheat	10	45.34

Salts and Copper Finings	
Item	**Grams**
DWB	1250
Copper Finings	14 tabs

Hops		
Hop	**Grams**	**Stage**
Admiral	1400	Aroma
Centennial	1000	Kettle
Simcoe	1500	Kettle
Amarillo	1500	Kettle
Centennial	750	Hop Basket
Simcoe	750	Hop Basket

Single Hop IPA 4.2%

A single hop session IPA.

Grist		
Malt	**%**	**KG**
Clear Choice Malt Ale	90	298.19
Torrified Wheat	10	35.11

Salts and Copper Finings	
Item	**Grams**
DWB	1250
Copper Finings	14 tabs

Hops		
Hop	**Grams**	**Stage**
Admiral	1300	Kettle
Jester	2500	Kettle
Jester	1200	Hop Basket
Jester	5000	Dry Hop in FV

Best Bitter 4.5%

The classic British Amber Ale.

Grist		
Malt	**%**	**KG**
Finest Maris Otter	88.3	286.02
Light Crystal (Crystal 150)	3	11.09
Medium Crystal (Crystal 240)	4.2	15.71
Torrified Wheat	4.5	15.53

Salts and Copper Finings	
Item	Grams
DWB	1250
Copper Finings	14 tabs

Hops		
Hop	**Grams**	**Stage**
Challenger	1000	Kettle
Goldings	800	Kettle
Northdown	800	Hop Basket
Fuggles	400	Aroma

Red Ale 4.6%

The combination of a bigger grist with fruity hops punch.

Grist		
Malt	**%**	**KG**
Finest Maris Otter	85	270.49
Dark Crystal (Crystal 400)	4	14.45
Medium Crystal (Crystal 240)	3	10.89
Brown Malt	2	7.02
Roast Barley	1	3.57
Torrified Wheat	5	16.95

Salts and Copper Finings	
Item	Grams
DWB	1250
Copper Finings	14 tabs

Hops		
Hop	Grams	Stage
Eagle	1000	Kettle
Nectaron	1500	Kettle
Amarillo	1000	Hop Basket
Simcoe	4000	Dry Hop in Vessel

Dark Beer 5%

A big flavoursome dark ale.

Grist		
Malt	**%**	**KG**
Finest Maris Otter® Ale Malt	50	176.97
Light Munich Malt	25.6	94.31
Medium Crystal (Crystal 240)	2.7	10.73
Dark Crystal (Crystal 400)	2.9	11.65
Brown Malt	2.7	10.85
Black Malt	3.8	15.34
Chocolate Malt	2.7	10.66
Cara Gold Malt	3.9	15.22
Roast Barley	1	3.98
Torrefied Wheat	2.8	10.56

| Cara Malt | 1.9 | 7.68 |

Salts and Copper Finings	
Item	**Grams**
DWB	1250
Copper Finings	14 tabs

Hops		
Hop	**Grams**	**Stage**
Admiral	1600	Kettle
Fuggles	1250	Kettle
Goldings	850	Kettle
Northdown	1350	Hop Basket

Glossary of Terms

All Those Beer Terms

Having read back the book we realised there's a few brewing terms in here that, although they might be second nature to us, everyone may not understand, so we decided to create a glossary.

- **ABV:** Alcohol By Volume. In essence, the alcoholic strength of the beer, for example 5% ABV.

- **Aroma Hops:** These are added at the end of the boil and add more fruity elements to the beer.

- **Bittering Hops:** The hops added at the start of the boil. The aim of these hops is to add bitterness to the beer.

- **Cask:** The term given to a barrel. These can be in 9- or 18-gallon size. All cask beer is filled into these at the final stage of the brew process.

- **Caustic:** A chemical used to clean the brewery, helping to sterilise the plant between brews. It must be flushed through with water afterwards.

- **CIP Spray Ball:** A rotating CIP ball used to clean brewing vessels.

- **Cold Store:** A giant cold room which is temperature controlled.

- **Copper:** A giant kettle, used to boil up the ingredients during the brewing process.

- **Copper Coils:** The coils in the bottom of the copper, much like the coils in the kettle. These heat up the liquid to reach boiling point and must be covered in liquid before the copper can be turned on.

- **Craft Cask:** A craft style cask ale.

- **Crop the Yeast:** The process of collecting some of the yeast from the top of the open topped fermentation vessel, to be used on subsequent brews.

- **Dry Hopping:** The process of adding hops to the beer at the later stages in order to add higher alpha fruity flavours to beer. These can be added at three stages, via the hop basket, in fermentation vessel, or in cask.

- **DWB:** The formula or blend of minerals provided by your brew chemist to make your water optimal for brewing. This would be added to your brew water prior to getting your mash in.

- **Fermentation Vessel or FV:** A large stainless-steel, temperature-controlled vessel, filled with the wort for the yeast to be added and convert those sugars into alcohol.

- **Free House:** A pub which is completely free to sell any beers they wish and has a large selection of beers from many different brewers. Historically, at the time of opening, the Brunswick brewers all had their own pubs and only sold their own beers. Which is why it was such a success with 17 hand pulls of beer from far and wide.

- **Grist:** The grist is your weighed out malt that forms the malt element of your recipe.

- **Hop Basket:** A round stainless-steel basket, with a wire mesh bottom housed in the underback and used to consistently dry hop the beer.

- **Hop Bible:** The term given to the brochure of hops that are available for all brewers to purchase from. This would include all the data on each hop, including profiles and alpha contents.

- **Hop Contract:** Hops are purchased up to three years in advance. This is the pre-agreed contract of the hops your brewery will purchase, which you are legally contracted to purchase.

- **Hop Pellets:** Hop pellets are produced from kiln dried whole hops, hammer milled into a powder and passed through a pellet die.

- **Hop Plugs:** Tiny hop bales designed for in-cask dry hopping.

- **Hot Liquor Tanks:** Temperature controlled tanks housing water at temperature, often used in the liquoring back process.

- **Liquoring Back:** The process of adding water to the wort if it's a higher density than is required.

- **Maltster:** The company or person who provides your malt ready to brew with. They would follow the full process from germination to roasting to provide the various malts available to a brewer and be used in their recipe.

- **Mash Tun:** The vessel used to mix your brew water and milled malt into a porridge. Typically, the vessel would have stainless steel plates above the bottom. These plates contain holes that allow liquid to pass through but not the malt. In effect, acting like a sieve.

- **Mash Water:** The term sometimes given to the water used for mashing in.

- **Mashing or Mashing In:** The process of hand turning the milled malt into your water to form a porridge like mixture.

- **Microbreweries:** The original term given to smaller artisan breweries.

- **Milling:** The process of lightly crushing the shell of the malt to allow the flavour to be infused into the water to form your wort.

- **Paddle:** A spade with holes is used to mix the milled malt with the brew water to form a porridge during the mash in process.

- **Paraflow:** Used to reduce the temperature of the beer from around 80 degrees to 18–20 degrees during collection. In order that the wort is at the required temperature for the yeast to flourish and convert the sugars to alcohol. The device is similar to a reverse radiator passing the hot wort in pipes very close to pipes with cold water to reduce its temperature.

- **Peracetic Acid:** A chemical used to sterilise brewing equipment and vessels. Once dry the item is sterile with no need to flush with water, so ready to use.

- **Percentage of Grist:** This is simply each element percentage of the total grist or malt in your recipe.

- **Raking:** The process of filling casks with beer.

- **Raking Tanks:** Large tanks with a thimble, used to allow the beer to settle, removing further yeast prior to barrelling.

- **Run Off:** The extraction of your wort from the mash. In our case, into the underback.

- **Sparging:** Lightly sprinkling water over the top of your mash or porridge like mixture.

- **Transfer:** The transfer of the hot wort from the underback to the fermentation vessel where yeast will be added to start the fermentation process.

- **Underback:** A large stainless-steel bath used in run off and collection.

- **Whole Hops:** The full hop flavour in its original form.

- **Wort:** The name given to the malt-infused liquid which, once fermented, will become your beer.

The End

We hope you have enjoyed reading the book as much
as we have writing it.

Cheers

Trev and Paul

Free Download

We hope you enjoyed learning the secrets to make great beer. To continue your journey with us, download our free guide to find the perfect beer to suit your tastes and explore something new. Scan the QR code below with your phone camera.

Leave A Review

If you enjoyed our book, please take a minute to leave us a 5 Star Review on Amazon. Scan the QR code below with your phone camera to take you directly to the review page.

Printed in Great Britain
by Amazon